NATIONAL PARKS MARKETING AND CONSERVATION SURVEY

Prepared by Fielder Green Associates
for the Countryside Commission

Distributed by:
Countryside Commission Publications
Printworks Lane
Levenshulme
Manchester M19 3JP
Telephone: 061-224 6287

© Countryside Commission 1992
ISBN 0 86170 315 4
CCP 354
Price £4.50

CONTENTS

Appendices

Figures

PREFACE

The relationship between tourism and the environment is of growing interest and concern, not least in our national parks, which are both fragile environments and popular destinations for visitors.

In 1989 the Countryside Commission concluded Heads of Agreement on tourism in national parks with the English Tourist Board and the Wales Tourist Board. These agreements consisted of a set of principles to guide the development of tourism and a programme of research and initiatives to find ways of involving the tourism industry in support of national park purposes. A particular issue identified was the need to investigate the level to which national parks are marketed by the tourism industry and the extent to which tourism operators already support conservation activities within the parks.

Fielder Green Associates was contracted in early 1990 to carry out this research. This report sets out their findings. The recommendations in chapters 15 and 17 have been endorsed by the steering group of officers overseeing the Heads of Agreement representing the Countryside Commission, Countryside Council for Wales, English Tourist Board, Wales Tourist Board, regional tourist boards and national park authorities. The steering group hopes that the information and recommendations in this report will assist national park authorities and the tourism industry in considering how best to market tourism in national parks in ways that produce conservation benefits.

Countryside Commission
December 1991

1. SUMMARY

The research described in this report is the result of a survey commissioned by the partners to the Heads of Agreement on tourism in national parks — the Countryside Commission and the English and Wales Tourist Boards.

Given the complex nature of marketing and the diverse range of businesses and organisations involved in the survey, it was agreed that research should concentrate on the 'promotion' aspects of marketing.

The research was carried out during 1990, using 1989 as a base year, and consisted of: establishing databases of tourism businesses operating in and near to national parks (6,000 businesses); a postal questionnaire, which generated a 24 per cent response rate and 60 face-to-face interviews with local authority, tourist board and national park officers (see section 3).

The consultants estimate that they were able to collect the names and addresses of 50–70 per cent of all tourism businesses operating in and near to national parks. An element of bias was introduced by the sources of these details (see section 4).

The most numerous group surveyed was 'tourism businesses', and these account for an estimated 90 per cent of all promotional spending that results in visits to national parks. The nature of this spending was similar from park to park, with slightly more noticeable differences between business types. Production and distribution of a brochure and advertising accounts for almost 80 per cent of business promotional spending. Little advice is sought by businesses during planning, and remarkably little monitoring of effectiveness is done.

Most businesses are aware of the dual objectives of national park authorities, and see their location in or near to a national park as a positive marketing factor (see section 6).

Local authorities are equally aware of national park objectives and see the national parks similarly as 'unique selling points'. Their objectives are broader than those of tourism businesses and consultation during promotional planning is much wider.

Print production and distribution account for the majority of local authority promotional spend and much of this is done with financial contributions from the commercial sector, or in partnership with businesses, other local authorities or tourist boards (see section 7).

National park authorities all carry out a range of 'tourism marketing' activities. Print production and distribution, the operation of visitor centres and guided walks and events programmes are common.

Although all of the parks are working to communicate identical messages, there is currently no 'corporate' promotion of the parks as a family, which we see as a lost opportunity. Consultation by parks on tourism marketing varies from park to park and within individual national park authorities, because the majority have no clear procedure and no clear allocation of responsibility (see section 8).

Regional tourist boards (and the regional offices of the Wales Tourist Board) incorporate national park objectives into their development and marketing strategies. The boards see the parks as unique selling points within 'regional' destination products. They communicate mainly pictorial messages about the parks. The boards have a sophisticated marketing function and carry out more monitoring and research than the local authorities or businesses (see section 9).

The importance of national parks reduces with distance from the park; a smaller proportion of promotional spending relates to national parks among organisations operating at national level, for example the British Tourist Authority (see sections 10 and 11).

Messages relating to the parks that are communicated by businesses and organisations are given a relatively low priority and are in most cases used to give a destination a 'quality of landscape' endorsement. Very few messages cover the special or fragile nature of the parks and the need to protect them (see section 13).

Promotional spending by businesses and organisations that results in visits to national parks is estimated to be £28,249,071 (in the region of 8 per cent of all such spending in England and Wales). Of this, 90 per cent is by businesses, most of the remainder by local authorities and regional tourist boards, and the rest by national park authorities and national organisations (see section 14).

Most businesses (80 per cent) give no support to conservation in national parks, with only 9 per cent giving financial support. Of those that do give, 60 per cent support conservation that they carry out themselves. Many businesses see the running of the business as a type of conservation. Of those that do not support conservation, a high proportion commented that they would like to do so, but do not know how, or had not been asked (see section 16).

The report makes recommendations on marketing (see section 15) and conservation support (see section 17). These contain suggestions for action which would:
- increase the involvement of national parks in tourism marketing and promotion that would occur regardless, thereby giving them the opportunity to influence its direction;
- increase the level of funds generated for conservation support in national parks from businesses and through businesses from their customers.

A statistical volume that contains detailed results of the survey is available from Fielder Green Associates (Tel: 0904 640650).

2. INTRODUCTION

Throughout the study, the consultants reported to a steering group made up of officers from the commissioning agencies and from national park authorities and regional tourist boards — the Tourism in National Parks Steering Group.

The agreed objectives of the study were as follows:

- **To determine the extent to which national parks are currently marketed, by whom and at what cost, and to judge the impact of current marketing initiatives.**
- **To appraise the nature of, and the messages underlying, current marketing initiatives and to judge them in relation to the *Principles for tourism in national parks* (see appendix 1).**
- **To identify potential marketing gaps at national and regional levels.**
- **To identify opportunities to realign existing marketing messages where they conflict with the character and culture of national parks.**
- **To ascertain the current level and nature of support for practical conservation measures from the tourism industry.**

The scope of the study was very wide as it needed to consider the activities of a large number of organisations from the private, public and voluntary sectors located in or near all of the national parks of England and Wales, as well as organisations located distant from the national parks, but which may carry out marketing activities that cause visits to national parks (for example tour operators and coach operators).

Because of the wide scope of both the study sample and marketing as a business discipline, it was decided by the project steering group that the marketing audit should concentrate its investigation on the more visible elements of the marketing mix, namely promotion. Other relevant areas of marketing are referred to where it is deemed necessary.

The study has been carried out in a context within which a number of dynamic factors have an effect on tourism and the national parks; these include the following.

- **Increasing affluence, mobility and leisure time** continues to cause an increase in tourism and day-trip demand.
- **Growing interest in, and appreciation of, environmental issues and 'natural' places** is causing a compounded increase in demand for tourism and day-trips to the countryside.
- **Increasing interest by tourist boards in visitor management and the concepts of sustainable and green tourism.**
- **Concern that the existing powers vested in national parks may no longer be adequate to achieve the national parks' objectives.**

Marketing is a management technique that has, to date, been given little attention by the majority of conservation and countryside management organisations in England and Wales. This is due in no small part to the association of the technique with profit. Increasingly, however, many of these organisations are learning that marketing can be employed to achieve objectives other than profit, including conservation, education and visitor management.

3. METHODOLOGY

The consultants employed a standard research theory for the exercise, which was as follows:
- establish research objectives;
- research secondary and primary data;
- establish research approach;
- develop sampling plan;
- collect data;
- analyse data.

The research objectives are described on page 5.

In order to create databases of tourism businesses, the consultants gathered together the names and addresses of tourism organisations and businesses, which included the following:
- tourist boards;
- county councils;
- district councils;
- national park authorities;
- tourism associations/consortia;
- accommodation providers;
- activity and study centres;
- visitor attractions;
- land owning organisations;
- tour operators;
- transport operators;
- miscellaneous services;
- voluntary organisations.

Each of the databases are divisible by national park and by location in, near, or distant from national parks. The exercise resulted in the collection of the addresses of almost 6,000 organisations and businesses (see appendix 2).

The sources of these names and addresses were tourist board and other tourism publications, local authority publications, national park publications, lists acquired from organisations, lists available from handbooks, the consultants' own existing databases and lists from other publications. The total was checked for duplication.

Given that the majority of data required was 'descriptive', a survey approach was chosen for the project. Two versions of a questionnaire were designed and printed; this was mailed to the contacts on the database, together with a freepost envelope for the reply.

The survey work was supplemented by face to face interviews with organisations, which enabled a more qualitative approach. For each national park, interviews were held with the national park authority, the regional tourist board and a selective sample of two local authorities. In addition, interviews were held with the national tourist boards and the Countryside Commission (see appendix 3).

A total of 1,446 completed questionnaires were received and processed (see appendix 2 for breakdown by national park and by respondent type). A data manipulation computer software package was used to enable the consultants to cross reference the answers to any question against the other questions, by respondent type, by park or by location in or near a park. The findings are reported in sections 6 to 9.

In order to evaluate the quality and nature of messages relating to the national parks, interviewees were asked to return a copy of their promotional literature along with their completed questionnaire. These were analysed against a set of criteria and the findings are described in section 13.

Summary

- **A database with 5,884 entries was produced. This was divisible by park, by organisation type and by location.**
- **A high response rate was achieved: 25 per cent, 1,446 questionnaires in all.**
- **The questionnaire was supplemented by interviews with representatives of tourist boards, local authorities, national park authorities and the national agencies.**

4. LIMITATIONS AND CONSTRAINTS

Variations in the methods employed for data collection have resulted in different emphases in the information collected from each park and by each organisation type; they are detailed in the report where relevant.

For the compilation of the databases, no comprehensive lists of organisations and businesses operating in and near the national parks were available. Although every effort was made to build the most comprehensive databases possible, the consultants feel that the databases used for the study represent between 50 and 70 per cent of tourism businesses in and near the national parks.

A fundamental bias is built into all of the figures. This is the result of the nature of the sources available for compiling the databases; since these were predominantly tourist related publications, the databases will be dominated by organisations and businesses that are more active in marketing themselves. Less professional and less conventional organisations, plus those that may intentionally be avoiding the established channels for other reasons (tax liability, etc) will not be represented in the databases to the same extent.

The above point relates almost exclusively to businesses, and it should be noted that the more professional and visible businesses will be achieving higher marketing impact and so are more relevant to this study.

Of the 5,884 organisations surveyed, a higher than expected response rate was achieved (24 per cent). This reflects the high interest in the subject. However, in order to calculate estimates for total spending and activities, the consultants had to extrapolate estimated total figures from this 24 per cent. There is a clear error potential in this extrapolation.

This is further complicated by the fact that the response rate by park, by geographical location and by operator or organisation type varies. In particular, we feel that the estimated figures for the Yorkshire Dales National Park (where the sample size, in relation to the number of businesses in and near to the park, was small) and for the Snowdonia National Park (where the response rate was low) should be treated with caution.

The three factors described above may result in inaccuracies in the estimated figures. We have been particularly aware of these error factors and have taken them into account at every stage of the study.

It is possible that a certain amount of individual bias was introduced into the discussion during the interviews. It was felt on some occasions that 'diplomatic' answers were given to certain questions. However, we feel that the results of the interviews have given a valuable qualitative aspect to the study.

It was intended to carry out a limited appraisal of press articles, publications and exposure of the national parks in other media. This was attempted, but the sources of information were found to be too broad and so inconsistently recorded as to render the exercise relatively meaningless. As a result it was not possible to fully research this field of activity, although public relations activity by the national parks and publications are covered in sections 8 and 13.

Summary

- **The results of the survey are biased by the nature of sources of data available to the consultants, which favour businesses and organisations that are promoting themselves.**
- **The total figures are based on a response rate of 24 per cent.**
- **Response rates vary from park to park, from organisation type to organisation type and from location to location.**
- **Some individual bias was detected in the face to face interviews.**

5. THE STRUCTURE OF TOURISM MARKETING

In order to fully understand the findings of the study, it is necessary to understand the basic structure of tourism marketing.

The various organisations and businesses that carry out tourism marketing relating to national parks can be divided into five categories: international, national, regional, sub-regional and local.

The international level is represented by the British Tourist Authority (BTA). Its main responsibility is the promotion of Britain to overseas visitors, which is undertaken through the BTA overseas offices.

At the national level there are four tourist boards for the United Kingdom: the English Tourist Board, the Northern Ireland Tourist Board, the Scottish Tourist Board and the Wales Tourist Board. In this study we are concerned with the English Tourist Board and the Wales Tourist Board.

Their functions include: policy advice, hotel classification, grant aid (Wales Tourist Board only), advice, development initiatives, marketing initiatives (including the management of national campaigns), training, research and provision of grant-in-aid and project funding to the regional tourist boards.

At the regional level in England, tourism development and marketing is the responsibility of the 12 regional tourist boards. The regional boards are autonomous regional bodies that are financed by a combination of grant-in-aid from the English Tourist Board, local authorities, and from the tourism industry within each region through commercial membership and joint marketing schemes.

The precise objectives of each board vary, although in general terms their aim is to maximise the benefits of tourism through the encouragement of tourism developments and the organisation of various marketing exercises.

In Wales the situation is similar, although there are no regional boards. The regional board role is fulfilled by the regional offices of the Wales Tourist Board (WTB) which until recently operated as the North,

Mid and South Wales Tourism Councils. The responsibilities of the WTB and its regional offices are similar to those of the ETB and its regional boards, although the WTB is still able to offer 'Section Four' development funding.

Sub-regionally, a number of different organisations carry out tourism marketing. The level of marketing activity and the levels of consultation and cooperation vary considerably in quantity and quality from region to region and from organisation to organisation within each region.

The organisations operating at this level consist mainly of county councils and district councils, which have the objective of optimising tourism revenue and jobs within their own boundaries; they achieve this by carrying out marketing and development activities. Some of these authorities have tourism departments, others have a tourism officer, most commonly located in either the planning, economic development or leisure services departments. It is sometimes the case that the county council plays an area coordinating role for the district councils.

A variety of tourism associations, groups and consortia exist around the country. These are often formed on the initiative or prompting of a local authority or regional tourist board, although their members are predominantly from the commercial sector. The structure, size, objectives and effectiveness of these organisations vary greatly.

The foundation of this tourism marketing structure is the many thousands of tourism businesses that make up the supply side of the industry. The tourism industry in general is made up of a very large number of small, independently owned businesses, with some larger businesses (for example hotel chains) that are organised on a national or international basis.

The small-scale nature of the majority of tourism businesses has resulted in a situation where limited marketing resources are applied in a fragmented way.

This section summarises the findings of the main questionnaire that was mailed to tourism businesses in or near to national parks.

Awareness of the dual objectives of national parks

The results show a high level of awareness of the national parks' joint aims of **conservation** and **promotion of public enjoyment** (see Figure 1).

Figure 1. Awareness of dual objectives

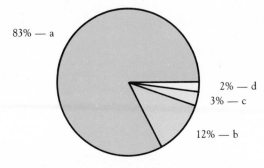

83% — a
2% — d
3% — c
12% — b

a: Conservation and public enjoyment
b: Conservation only
c: Promotion of public enjoyment only
d: Allows the Government to purchase scenic land

Variations in these results between different regions and business types are fairly insignificant, and are probably a result of sampling rather than any major influencing factor.

Importance of location in or near to a national park

More than three-quarters of the sample felt that their location in or near to a national park was of benefit to the operation of their business: 17 per cent of the sample felt it was 'essential' to their business, while only 3 per cent felt that it 'hindered' (see Table 1).

This was the expected result, although it might have been thought that 'hinders' would have featured more prominently in the total sample because of the often publicised detrimental effects of designation, eg tighter planning controls on businesses.

Regionally, above average scores for 'essential' were recorded from Exmoor, the Peak District and the Lake District, while the Broads and Northumberland returned higher 'no difference' scores.

This noticeable variance is probably the result of different levels of public awareness of the different parks. For example, the Broads, which has been

Table 1. The importance of location: selected parks compared with total sample.

Importance	Total sample (%)	Exmoor (%)	Peak District (%)	Lake District (%)	Broads (%)	Northum-berland (%)
Essential	17	26	26	28	6	2
Helps	69	65	65	63	60	67
Makes no difference	11	9	2	2	32	31
Hinders	3	0	7	7	2	0

designated more recently, enjoys lower public awareness of its status than, say, the Lake District.

Promotional advice and assistance: the extent of consultation

The level of consultation by tourism businesses when designing promotional literature is low, with 56 per cent of the sample seeking no advice on promotional planning (see Table 2). Of those that do consult, 64 per cent approach their respective regional tourist board. Understandably, very few businesses use the national park authorities as a source of promotional advice.

The relatively high percentages of consultation with regional tourist boards, county councils and district councils reflect their coordination of joint publications and joint promotions with the local tourism industry.

Fewer businesses 'in' national parks conduct consultation than those 'near to' national parks, and there is no significant difference in the number seeking advice from a national park authority (Figure 2). The low level of consultation is felt to be consistent with the tourism industry in general.

Type of promotional activities undertaken

Brochure and leaflet production, their distribution and their advertisement is undertaken by the majority of the sample.

Activities that directly or indirectly involve regional tourist boards feature prominently, eg tourist guide advertising and tourist board membership.

The more specialist marketing activities, such as public relations, exhibitions and coordinated marketing activities through consortia or groups, are not common.

Regionally, there are a number of noticeable deviations from the overall pattern, as follows:

Table 2. Promotional consultation: selected parks compared with total sample†.

Organisation consulted by businesses during promotional planning	Total sample (%)	Of those that consult (%)	Northumberland (%)	Snowdonia (%)	Broads (%)	Exmoor (%)	Lake District (%)
Regional tourist board	28	64	41	53	20	19	26
National park	6	13	12	1	3	8	2
County council	10	22	24	12	6	12	6
District council	17	38	24	16	17	8	13
Tourism association	9	22	11	19	8	14	7
None	56	–	48	41	52	57	67

Figure 2. Promotional consultation: a comparison between those businesses located 'in' and 'near' a national park.

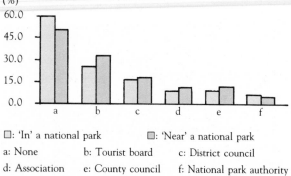

(%)

☐: 'In' a national park   ☐: 'Near' a national park

a: None   b: Tourist board   c: District council
d: Association   e: County council   f: National park authority

- the Broads has a lower level of regional tourist board membership;
- Dartmoor has a higher level of marketing group membership;
- more businesses in the Northumberland region participate in press related activities.

A comparison of attractions and accommodation units shows particular differences in the approaches of the two groups to promotion (Table 3). Attractions place greater emphasis on print production, newspaper and magazine advertising, public relations and exhibitions, while accommodation units undertake more regional tourist board membership and

Table 3. Breakdown of spending on promotion by selected business types.

	Attractions (%)	Accommodation providers (%)	Activity managers (%)
Print	34	20	34
Distribution	6	5	7
Advertising	35	55	43
Public relations	3	*	3
Exhibitions	3	*	2
Posters and Signs	6	3	5
Other	13	17	6
TOTAL	100	100	100

*Less than 0.5%

†In some cases, the answers to the questions in the questionnaire were not mutually exclusive. This means that in those cases totals are in excess of 100%.

tourist guide advertising. Activity centres also vary from the pattern, showing similar characteristics to attractions.

Allocation of promotional expenditure

Of the total promotional spend, almost half is allocated to advertising, and nearly a third is allocated to brochure and leaflet production and distribution (Figure 3).

Figure 3. Allocation of promotional expenditure by tourism businesses.

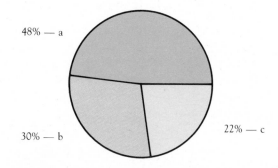

48% — a

30% — b

22% — c

a: Advertising
b: Brochure and leaflet production and distribution
c: Other (various activities that individually do not exceed 8 per cent of total spending)

Participation in joint promotional activities

Most tourism businesses do not participate in joint promotional activities (64 per cent of those sampled). Of those that do:

- 20 per cent of the total sample participate with a tourist board;
- 13 per cent participate with a local authority;
- 8 per cent participate with an accommodation unit.

The regional tourist boards and local authorities will undoubtedly have taken the lead in most of these joint activities. This is not uncommon among tourism businesses, as smaller businesses often view other businesses as competition, rather than as potential partners in a destination marketing exercise.

This pattern does not vary significantly between regions. Attractions undertake more joint activities, often in the form of joint print and joint admission tickets with each other and packaging with tour operators.

Target markets

Only 6 per cent of the sample admitted that they did not target their promotion. Of those that did, 78 per cent targeted 'main holiday tourists' and 68 per cent targeted 'short-break tourists' (Table 4).

Regionally, there are a few noticeable differences, as follows:
- the Broads — less targeting of overseas tourists;
- the Brecon Beacons — greater overseas aiming;
- the Peak District — less main holiday and increased targeting of day trippers;
- the Yorkshire Dales — greater targeting of short-break tourists.

Comparisons between types of businesses show a noticeable difference between attractions and accommodation units: as could be expected, attractions target visitors in the park, day trippers and coach/tour operators, which means that their promotion is geographically more concentrated.

Monitoring of success

Very little monitoring of promotional activities takes place in the national parks:
- 22 per cent of businesses do no monitoring;
- 60 per cent asked visitors informally and 37 per cent counted visitor numbers;
- only 8 per cent conducted a 'formal' visitor survey;
- only 9 per cent ran a coded voucher/advertisement scheme.

This is a disappointing result, but one not inconsistent with the national situation. It is especially surprising considering that at least 80 per cent of businesses took part in some form of advertising.

Promotional success

Measured on a scale of 1 to 5 (with '1' being very successful and '5' being very unsuccessful), most tourism businesses surveyed (43 per cent of the total sample) opted for the middle line and chose '3' (see Figure 4).

This suggests that these businesses considered their promotional activities to be neither successful nor unsuccessful. However, it must be said that the middle line may have been seen as implying 'average' success by some of the businesses.

Figure 4. Promotional success.

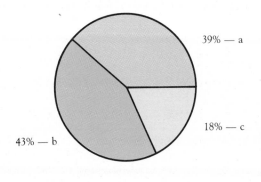

39% — a

18% — c

43% — b

a: Successful
b: Neither successful nor unsuccessful
c: Unsuccessful

Summary

- **The vast majority of tourism businesses are aware of the national parks' dual objectives and feel that their location in or near to a national park benefits the operation of their business.**
- **Most businesses produce a brochure and advertise, and the vast majority of promotional budgets are spent on these activities.**
- **Few ask for advice on these activities and few participate in joint activities.**
- **Businesses generally know who they are directing their promotion at, which is still led by traditional main holiday tourists.**
- **Only a minority of businesses feel that they are successful in their promotion, yet very few formally monitor their activities.**

Table 4. Target markets for promotional activities: selected regions compared with total sample.

Targets	Total sample	The Broads	Brecon Beacons	Peak District	Yorkshire Dales	Attractions	Accommodation
	(%)	(%)	(%)	(%)	(%)	(%)	(%)
Main holiday tourists	78	79	78	51	77	80	80
Short break tourists	68	58	67	71	83	68	69
Overseas visitors	40	25	67	36	36	46	39
Visitors in national park	27	13	33	39	37	56	19
Day trippers	22	22	22	35	28	64	9
Coach/tour operators	12	8	14	15	8	36	7

7. LOCAL AUTHORITIES

Introduction

Local authorities whose areas overlap national parks were sent a questionnaire. There was a high rate of response. In addition, a number of interviews were held with selected local authority tourism officers (see appendix 3).

The quantity and quality of tourism promotion carried out by local authorities varies considerably, as do the following:
- their objectives for tourism promotion;
- their level of expertise;
- the level of resources allocated to tourism promotion;
- their attitudes to tourism and the national parks.

Tourism objectives

Local authority objectives for tourism (development and marketing) are concentrated on the provision of jobs and increasing visitor spending. Some authorities stated 'to increase visitor numbers' as an objective.

Tourism departments of local authorities are responsible first to their members and to policy objectives for tourism, spending and job creation before accounting for the objectives of other organisations such as the national park authorities.

A number of authorities have incorporated the objectives (and visitor management objectives) of the national parks into their own tourism strategies (eg Brecknock Borough Council, Brecon Beacons), while others take little or no account of these at all (eg Richmondshire District Council, Yorkshire Dales).

Awareness of national park objectives

Awareness of national park objectives is accurate among local authority tourism officers, although in a number of cases understanding was quoted 'in broad terms'.

The objective of all authorities interviewed was to promote tourism to the whole county/district, not just a part of it, and a number of authorities had as a specific objective 'to spread the benefits of tourism throughout the county/district'.

Quantitative results show that 89 per cent of the local authorities are aware of the dual objectives of the national parks: this is higher than tourism businesses (83 per cent), although a number of authorities (11 per cent) see the national parks as being solely conservation orientated.

The importance of location in or near to a national park

The vast majority of local authorities view the existence of national parks in or close to their areas as a positive factor in achieving their tourism objectives (Figure 5).

Figure 5. Importance of location for local authorities.

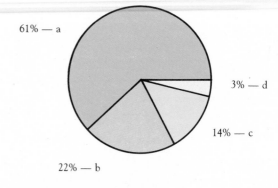

61% — a
3% — d
14% — c
22% — b

a: It helps tourism promotion
b: It is essential to tourism promotion
c: It makes no difference to tourism promotion
d: It hinders tourism promotion

National parks are seen by most local authorities as just one of a range of tourism products that they have on offer. It is sometimes seen as a promotional 'carrot' to attract tourists to stay in other parts of the area.

The importance of national parks as a promotional tool reduces as local authorities create their own destination product identities. Ryedale is a typical example; approximately 30 per cent of the area of the North York Moors National Park lies within the boundary of Ryedale District Council, and the park has always been seen as an important part of the district's tourism product. Ryedale District Council has recently invested considerable resources in the development and promotion of a new image for the district — 'Ryedale; The Quest'. This has been successful and as a result the park has become a less important factor in promotion of the district.

This pattern will become more common as local authorities strive to create strong identities for themselves.

Promotional consultation

The level of communication and consultation between local authorities and other organisations is high: only 3 per cent of the total sample (ie one authority) admitted to no consultation at all.

More than 80 per cent of local authorities asked for advice or assistance from their regional tourist board and nearly half consulted their national park authority (Table 5).

Table 5. Promotional consultation: local authorities.

Organisation	Local authorities (%)
Regional tourist board	81
District council	62
County council	51
Tourism association	49
National park authority	46
Other (specified)	24
Private consultant	16

Consultation by local authorities on marketing planning was varied. In most regions regular consultation takes place with the regional tourist boards, often through tourism officers' groups, or through coordinating county councils.

Consultation with national park authorities is similarly varied and ranges from 'total disregard' to 'very close'. For example, the tourism officer of Brecknock Borough Council regards the borough's destination product boundary as being synonymous with that of the Brecon Beacons National Park and so 'consults the national park authority at all stages regarding marketing'.

Few tourism officers had conflicts with the national park authorities on the subject of marketing, although the subject of development is more likely to lead to conflict.

Local authorities often act as a link between the promotion activities of the regional tourist boards and the commercial sector. In some cases the county councils play a coordinating role for the districts, who work together on county-wide promotions, for example, the Somerset Tourism Initiative led by Somerset County Council.

Gwynedd County Council, for example, channels most of its tourism promotion funding and time resources (except that allocated to tourist information centres) through the district council tourism departments; its tourism officer liaises with, and coordinates the efforts of, the districts. Some county councils, for example North Yorkshire, have no tourism marketing function at all; they channel their efforts through the regional tourist board.

Several local authority tourism officers stated that they had been given conflicting messages on the same subject by different individuals within a national park authority. Many felt that the nature of communication was subject to the personal interpretations of the individual national park officer consulted.

Consultation fora

Local authorities play an important role in the many tourism consultation fora that have been set up around national park areas expressly for the purpose of increasing communication between the national park authorities and the tourism industry, or as a focus for joint and carefully managed tourism developments.

Promotional activities undertaken

Most local authorities undertake a wide range of marketing and promotional activities.

Table 6. Types of promotional activities undertaken by local authorities.

	%		%
Print		**PR**	
Accommodation guide	87	Host press visits	73
Atttraction guide	51	Press releases	65
Travel trade manual	46		
Specialist	46	**Other**	
Short-break guide	38	Attend exhibitions	84
		Tourist board member	78
Distribution		Join a marketing group	49
To tourist information centres	78	Other	41
By direct mail	65	Form a marketing group	35
Other	19	Display posters	30
		Display signs	27
Advertising		Run training courses	27
Tourist guide	78	Offer marketing grants	24
Magazine	76	Run an advice hotline	16
Newspaper	70		

Most of these activities are undertaken in partnership with other organisations or businesses in the region; for example, publishing destination brochures with paid insertions by tourism businesses, and organising an exhibition with attendance as a consortium or with commercial sector input.

Some marketing initiatives by local authorities are intended to attract visitors out of national parks. South Lakeland District Council (which has areas of the Lake District and the Yorkshire Dales National Parks within its boundaries) has three such initiatives:

- a car trail of the Furness area;
- a medium/long-distance footpath in the Furness area;
- an imaginative package called 'The grand tour', which combines steamer, rail and minibus transport.

Allocation of promotional expenditure

Print production and distribution costs account for nearly half of all local authority promotional expenditure. Advertising takes approximately one-fifth of promotional budgets, the rest being spent on other activities. This pattern is quite different from the more polarised expenditure of tourism businesses (see section 6).

Figure 6. Total local authority expenditure on promotional activities.

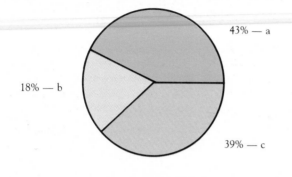

a: Brochure production and distribution
b: Various advertising expenditure
c: Other (various activities that individually do not exceed 10 per cent of total spending)

Joint promotional activities

Most promotional activities undertaken by local authorities are joint activities. Local authorities act as coordinators in some projects, while in others they are paying participants.

Three-quarters of the sample participated with a tourist board or another local authority. More than a third (36 per cent) of local authorities claim to take part in promotional activities with a national park authority.

Marketing messages

National parks are seen as positive promotional assets to most of the local authorities surveyed in this study. Most authorities said that they used the parks' qualities and the term 'national park' in their promotion.

The national park name is used to convey a quality landscape, and is often seen as a certificate or qualification of scenic beauty; this is particularly important in overseas promotion.

A number of authorities said that they did not communicate messages about the national park itself in their promotion, but that they did communicate messages about the geographical area (eg 'Lakeland' rather than the 'Lake District National Park').

Target markets

Local authorities were asked to rank their target markets in order of importance. Nearly two-thirds (61 per cent) place coach and tour operators as their number one target market.

Table 7. Local authority target markets, ranked in order of importance.

Target markets	1st (%)	2nd (%)	3rd (%)	4th (%)	5th (%)
Day trippers	14	42	42	3	0
Short-break tourists	6	41	22	19	11
Main holiday	6	11	14	42	28
Overseas	14	3	11	28	44
Coach and tour operators	61	3	11	8	17

Low priority is given to main holiday and short-break tourists. This is in stark contrast to tourism businesses, which target these groups.

Targeting by local authorities varied. Some authorities feel that they are on such restricted budgets that they 'cannot afford the luxury of targeting', being content with the provision of basic visitor information. However, most authorities stated that they 'target a range of markets that are consistent with the product they have on offer'.

Monitoring of success

Some monitoring is undertaken by local authorities; only 11 per cent of the sample admitted to carrying out no monitoring whatsoever. Of those that do monitor:

- 46 per cent count visitor numbers;
- 43 per cent ask visitors informally;
- 41 per cent run a coded advertisement scheme;
- only 22 per cent run any sort of formal visitor survey.

A lack of resources was most frequently quoted as the major constraint to monitoring.

District councils relied more often on informal feedback from accommodation units and attractions, while county councils tended to play a more prominent role in collecting tourism data.

All local authorities were conscious of the need for increased and more effective monitoring. They are becoming increasingly 'accountable', and will need to produce more accurate monitoring data in the future.

Promotional success

Local authorities were more confident about the success of their promotional activities than tourism businesses; 60 per cent of the sample felt that their activities were successful, while only 11 per cent felt that they were unsuccessful.

Figure 7. Local authorities' opinion of the success of their promotional activities.

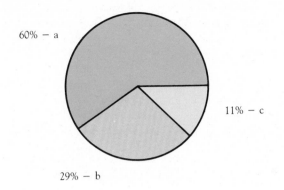

60% — a

11% — c

29% — b

a: Successful
b: Neither successful nor unsuccessful
c: Unsuccessful

Summary

- Local authorities promote tourism because it creates jobs and contributes to economic well-being.
- Local authorities understand the dual objectives of the national parks.
- Location in or partly in a national park is seen as a positive promotional factor.
- Promotional consultation is varied both in quantity and quality, but many authorities are involved in consultation fora and groups.
- Authorities undertake a variety of promotional activities, most in partnership with other organisations or businesses.
- Brochure production and distribution account for the majority of spending.
- Promotion is targeted widely, but coach and tour operators feature prominently.
- Monitoring is relatively poor, although this will improve due to increasing external pressure.
- Most authorities feel that their promotion is successful.

Attitudes towards statutory objectives

All national park authorities (NPAs) and the Broads Authority have the same statutory remit. They are affected and influenced by different local conditions. All 11 have the dual objectives of **conserving landscape** and **promoting public enjoyment**, and in doing so take account of the social and economic needs of their communities.

The word 'promotion' in statutory objectives is interpreted in slightly different ways in different parks; there are no clear national guide-lines. Many officers have difficulty in dealing with the word 'promotion', but most see it as promotion of 'responsible', 'respectful' or 'appropriate' tourism.

All NPAs conform to the Sandford principle and put conservation before tourism where there is an irreconcilable conflict between the two.

Actual tourism policy

National park authorities have all had to develop and publicise a tourism policy. This is often described by the broader term, recreation. The policies are similar in tone and essentially refer to the promotion and/or facilitation of 'suitable' or 'responsible' recreation and tourism that has due regard to the park's conservation. Below are a selection of examples to illustrate this point.

Brecon Beacons

"The NPA will promote the enjoyment of the park by the public engaging in suitable recreation activities", p 70, *National Park Plan*, first review, 1987.

The Broads

" . . . facilitating the use of the area for recreation and holiday purposes . . ." This aim is closely related to the embracing theme of protecting the special environment of the Broads, p 67, *Broads Plan*, 1987.

Lake District

"The NPA sees its role not to promote the tourism industry but to ensure that developments within the park do not prejudice those very qualities that originally were the industry's *raison d'être* . . . concerns are to maintain the character and promote quiet enjoyment . . . not to maximise the income from tourism". Chapter 11, p 2, *Lake District National Park Plan*, 1986.

North York Moors

"[The NPA] will support those forms of tourism development which do not threaten the special character of the National Park. Tourism promotion and development will be resisted where it conflicts with conservation objectives . . .", p 84, *North York Moors National Park Plan*, second review, 1990.

Attitudes towards tourism

Attitudes towards tourism and its marketing vary not only between individual parks but also between individual personalities within the park authorities. National park authority policies are fairly broad and allow personal interpretation. Below are a selection of quotes from the interviews undertaken for the study.

Brecon Beacons

"We quite happily accept that tourism exists and that it is part of the economy . . . but 'promotion' does not mean the National Park Authority is to go out and actively sell the park."

Dartmoor

"We are guarded about 'blanket' promotion . . . selective promotion will help to meet National Park Authority objectives."

Exmoor

"Section 86 of the Act is rather specific, but could be interpreted as requiring us to do pure selling . . . If the park is being promoted, then we see part of our responsibility as being to ensure the promotion is correct."

Attitudes towards marketing

Attitudes among national park authorities towards marketing vary noticeably; understanding, experience and training in the field are consistently low.

Some national park authorities, for example Northumberland, view marketing as 'difficult', and see the technique as a negative management tool, a useful device to control and deflect visitors. Other NPAs, for example Snowdonia, see marketing as 'necessary', while the Lake District NPA has grasped the value of the technique and applies it to the best of its resources.

Tourism marketing responsibility

The tourism and marketing function is usually handled by the information and interpretation section of

NPAs. Responsibility for this area is usually only a part of an individual's job, or may be spread among a number of individuals.

It is interesting to note the variety of contacts designated by the individual NPAs for this project (see appendix 3). Contacts included Principal Planning Officer, Information Officer and Deputy National Park Officer.

The North York Moors National Park is the only NPA to have appointed a Tourism and Recreation Officer, who's remit is to become involved in the park's tourism and recreation industry. The officer has been in post since February 1990 and is taking an active role in encouraging tourism and recreation that is consistent with park aims. To achieve this, the officer is engaged in a variety of activities, including:

- attending tourism officers' group meetings, organised by the regional tourist board and attended by county and district tourism officers;
- promoting the Captain Cook Tourism Association;
- organising a 'tourism forum' for the park, in order to explain the role of the park to tourism businesses and organisations and to encourage joint initiatives.

This appointment has been greeted with unanimous approval by the tourism departments of local authorities in the area and by the regional tourist board.

Promotional activities

All parks carry out a range of marketing activities. In general terms, the objectives for these activities are:

- to raise public awareness of the national park;
- to aid visitor management;
- to increase public enjoyment;
- to increase public understanding of the park's environment and its conservation;
- to generate public support for the national park.

Each park carries out its own marketing and communications activities. At the time of writing there were no national tourism marketing activities involving all 11 national parks.

Print production

Print production receives the greatest attention, with most NPAs publishing a large range of publications. These publications fall into two broad categories.

- Promotion and information print items, which are produced with the objectives of maximising public enjoyment and managing visitors by attracting them to particular sites (these are usually free of charge and usually carry a conservation message).
- Technical information print items intended for special interest groups, for which a charge is usually made.

To produce publications of a high quality, to reflect the high quality of the landscape within national parks, is an objective common to all NPAs.

National park newspapers

Annual newspapers are produced by eight of the parks. They are not produced in parks where the tourism industry is not large enough to support such a publication, for example Northumberland and the Brecon Beacons. The Broads Authority does not produce a newspaper because it feels that the medium is not consistent with the quality image it likes to communicate through its print items.

Newspapers are produced in huge quantity (for example the 250,000 print run of the *Lake District Guardian* and 200,000 print run of the *Exmoor Visitor*) and have an intense distribution within and close to national parks. They are also used for external promotion, being posted out in response to general information enquiries.

The newspapers are multi-purpose and are financed by the large amount of advertising that they carry. Each contains feature articles about the park and the NPA's activities, along with details of events and guided walks. Some contain formal accommodation and attraction guides.

By their nature the newspapers are 'throw away' items that have a short life-span. They are, however, cheap to produce, and some make a modest profit for the NPAs, which contract out production to local newspaper companies.

Park leaflets

Most parks have a general information leaflet of some kind, which contains an awareness, a conservation, and a directional message. Distribution varies; it includes visitor information centres in and near the parks (and, in the case of the Peak District, in large cities that surround the park) and is often sent out in response to information enquiries.

Accommodation guides

Accommodation guides are produced by some NPAs, either individually or as joint ventures. This is done where the NPA feels that accommodation information in one or more sectors is inadequate, for example the Lake District caravans and tents guide (single-sector) and the Brecon Beacons accommodation guide (all-sector).

Self-guided walking leaflets

Self-guided walking leaflets are produced by most NPAs, usually as a priced publication sold through visitor centres and other outlets.

Distribution

Distribution of print items varies subject to the nature of each publication — events guides and guided walks programme guides usually have a distribution limited to the park boundaries, or just outside, while general leaflets may go further. In a number of cases, including the North York Moors, the newspaper, although designed as an information item for visitors in the park, is often used to service enquiries from a distance, because there is no other suitable information available.

In some cases the distribution method does not appear to be matched closely to the use or objective of the print item. The Yorkshire Dales National Park accommodation guide, for example, is mainly distributed within the park, with only 2,000 copies of a 10,000 print run being distributed outside the park, from where the bulk of the demand for this service would come.

Advertising

Advertising has a low profile because resources are limited, even though the quality and accuracy of messages communicated by advertising are much more controllable than those communicated through public relations activities (which receive a higher spend allocation). Most advertising by NPAs is focused on openings or events and is placed in local news press or tourist guides.

An exception is Exmoor, where the NPA plans to take a double-page advert in the Exmoor tourism guide with the objective of attracting staying visitors from higher socio-economic groups.

Public relations

Public relations activities (for the purpose of this report, the sending of press releases, and the hosting of journalist and press events) are carried out by all NPAs, but in different ways. The levels of experience, expertise and resources available vary from park to park and tend to determine the level and quality of activity.

All parks carry out reactive public relations, but few are proactive on anything but a very localised scale, for example sending press releases and inviting journalists from the local news press to an opening, launch or other event. Most local press contact tends to be concerned with development and planning issues.

Some NPAs do engage in proactive public relations, for example the North York Moors NPA, which sends two-weekly press information sheets to a press mailing list and has developed working relationships with a number of media contacts, and Northumberland NPA, which systematically communicates with journalists.

The effects of PR activities are less predictable than those of advertising and other marketing activities. There are no guarantees that the media will pick up on stories. The media will often only feature items that are news-worthy (very subjective) or have a popular angle; for example Ryedale District Council (North

Yorkshire Moors National Park area) has run a successful PR campaign to raise the profile of the area. This programme has been based on a series of gimmick weekend breaks, such as 'A room with a moo' and 'Bog breaks'. This approach is not one that NPAs or their partners would want to follow, as this type of hype is often in conflict with the image that parks want to develop.

A number of NPAs run press-cutting services to monitor the coverage given to their park, mostly in local newspapers; the North York Moors, for example, have a cutting service run by the local authority. However, most parks do not currently take press cuttings systematically, nor do they use the information clipped.

Public relations activity is universally considered by the park authorities to be a cost-effective method of communicating with the public, and many parks felt that more resources and experience were needed in this area.

Contact with commercial publishers

A large number of commercial publications feature the 11 national parks. The NPAs have varying degrees of contact with publishers and authors. Most are, or have been, approached by writers, editors or publishers to comment or advise on facts for forthcoming publications.

This contact is *ad hoc* in nature and there are no set procedures for handling it. All officers agreed that this contact represents only a small number of publications produced annually, although most felt that this was an important, if not large scale, form of contact.

National park logos

All national parks have a logo; they are used on a variety of promotional items, ranging from boundary signs to merchandised products (such as sweatshirts) and print items.

Most were designed during the early stages of designation and are now looking rather out of date. The logos are also very individualistic, giving no indication of the existence of a 'family' of parks.

The importance of corporate identity has been recognised by the Peak District NPA, which has recently undergone a corporate identity review that resulted in the production of an up-dated logo that the NPA now intends to apply to all of its activities.

Product development

Some initiatives involving product development are carried out by NPAs. These include:

- the Hadrian's Wall bus service, which is supported by Northumberland National Park;
- guided walks programmes — operated by most parks — which offer more in-depth communication;
- conservation holidays produced and promoted by the North York Moors National Park — the authority is now hoping to pass on the handling operation to a local business;
- a combined guided walk and coach transport package from Newcastle, operated by Northumberland National Park with a local coach operator.

Target markets

Most of the marketing activities of the NPAs are aimed very broadly at all visitors, rather than being targeted at specific groups. This follows the 'national parks for everyone' thinking. Some parks target specific products or promotions at particular groups; for example, Exmoor NPA with its advertising, Lake District NPA with its camping and caravan guide, and Snowdonia NPA, which keeps some walking and information leaflets 'under the counter' to be given only to those who ask for them.

Merchandising

Most NPAs engage in merchandising, with the objectives of:
- generating revenue;
- increasing communication with the public by sending visitors home with a souvenir that carries a national park message.

Other objectives recorded were in the Broads, where the Broads Authority hoped to improve the quality of souvenirs available in the area and encourage other producers to emulate the authority's own standards, and in the Brecon Beacons, where one objective was to make a visitor centre more appealing by introducing an additional range of products.

The Yorkshire Dales National Park has placed its print production and merchandising functions under the responsibility of a limited company that is owned by the park. It will be interesting to see whether or not this venture is able to combine successfully financial and interpretative objectives, or whether items produced become more commercially attractive and less effective at communicating national park messages.

Most NPAs stated that they had no clear policy for merchandising, a number were uneasy about the issue, and almost all would benefit from or requested guidance on the subject.

Information centres

The operation of information centres is a means of communicating with a very large number of visitors to national parks. Monitoring suggests, for example, that 15 per cent of the 20 million visitors per annum to the Lake District National Park use one of the park's information centres.

All NPAs operate their own information centres, and a number are operated jointly by the NPAs and either a local authority, voluntary organisation (for example the National Trust) or business (for example, the Northumberland National Park and Northumbrian Water, and the Dartmoor National Park and South West Water).

The role of visitor centres within national parks varies. In the North York Moors National Park, for example, the three information centres have quite different roles:
- The Moors Centre is primarily an educational resource;
- The Sutton Bank Centre is part interpretative and part tourist information centre;
- Helmsley TIC is a tourist information centre.

Study centres

Two national parks have residential study centres — the Peak District (Losehill Hall) and Snowdonia (Plas Tan Y Bwlch). These give the NPA the opportunity to communicate in an in-depth way with individuals and groups that have special interests, with professionals in countryside management (through training courses) and with organisations (through conferences and seminars). The Lake District National Park will soon open the revamped Blencathra Youth Hostel as a study centre with similar objectives.

The original intention was that all national parks should have such a centre to enable this type of in-depth communication, and to act as a focus for research, interpretation, etc.

Consultation structure

Consultation on marketing issues by NPAs with other organisations and with businesses is inconsistent from park to park and, within each NPA, from department to department and from individual to individual. A range of consultation structures exist, ranging from various tourism associations, the Peak District Forum (a discussion forum for public sector organisations), to a Tourism Development Action Programme (TDAP) (in Dartmoor, where the NPA finances 25 per cent of the programme and chairs the officers' group), and the Exmoor Tourism Advisory Group, which developed out of a TDAP.

Most national parks consult only on an *ad hoc* basis and rely very much on the cross-committee positions of their board members, supplementing this by reactive consultation at officer level.

This situation often leads to the emission of confusing messages; for example, those received by South Lakeland District Council, which has regular contact with both the Lake District and Yorkshire Dales National Parks and which often receives quite different messages from each park on the same issues. The situation is rendered more difficult for the national park authorities, as they need to communicate with many different types of organisations.

Summary

- All NPAs are working towards the same statutory objectives, but interpretations vary, especially of the term 'promotion'.
- Responsibility for tourism and tourism marketing is often allocated to officers who also have other duties. The North York Moors, where a tourism officer has been appointed, is the exception.
- All NPAs carry out a range of tourism marketing activities, which are dominated by print production. A park newspaper and leaflet are the most common publications.
- There is very little targeting of marketing activities.
- Merchandising is common to all parks, but objectives, effectiveness and expertise vary.
- All NPAs run information and visitor centres, which communicate with visitors in a variety of ways and sometimes at different levels.
- NPAs are involved in a number of different consultation structures; the extent and influence of the NPA varies between each park and each structure.

Interviews were held with the marketing managers of all of the English regional tourist boards and the north and south regional offices of the Wales Tourist Board. These organisations were also asked to complete a form relating to activities carried out and allocation of marketing budgets.

Budgets, expertise and attitudes towards national parks were found to vary from board to board, although the boards consistently marketed an entire region as a 'destination product', as well as marketing individual products on a region-wide basis.

Since the boards market a region as a whole, it was not possible to determine accurately the amount of marketing spend per board that relates directly to the national parks.

Attitudes to national parks

The regional tourist boards were mostly aware of the dual objectives of the national parks and some were also aware of their social and economic reponsibilities to their communities. Most seemed to give the conservation objective greater importance.

The East Anglia Tourist Board was the least clear, quoting the fact that 'the Broads have only recently been given national park status' as a reason. Most boards were conscious of actual or potential conflict between themselves and the national park authorities, but did not see this as a problem because existing consultation procedures had led to a situation where national park objectives were accounted for in regional tourist board strategies. The boards all saw the national parks as 'special cases' because they are 'environmentally sensitive' and, as was the view of the East Midlands Tourist Board, 'because a large number of authorities and organisations consider them special'.

All national parks were using the national parks in their marketing as 'unique selling points'. The term 'national park' was felt by many to be an endorsement or qualification of the statements used in promotional print relating to scenic landscape.

Much of the information on national parks communicated to the public by the tourist boards is in pictorial form, especially scenic views and attractive villages.

Consultation

All boards consult with national park authorities, but the nature of the consultation varies. Most boards consult the national park authorities on the same level as they consult local authorities or regional offices of national agencies. Most send draft strategies and initiatives to national park authorities for comment, but if no comments are received the boards do not have the resources to chase, and the onus is on the NPA to respond. Most boards referred to consultation through cross-committee memberships, although pointed out that this was rather *ad hoc*.

Section 12 covers a number of specific consultation examples including the North York Moors Tourism Officer, the Dartmoor and Exmoor TDAPs and the Peak District Forum, which form a focus for consultation. Outside these areas, most boards felt that consultation was inadequate.

The example of the East Midlands Tourist Board was not unique; here the board's marketing manager regularly speaks to three individuals in the national park authority: "One often wonders who is looking after tourism — it would be useful [to have one appointed person] because then you would know where you were".

The Yorkshire & Humberside Tourist Board received conflicting messages from the Yorkshire Dales National Park Authority due to a change in policy mid-way through a project. The NPA originally supported (financially) a short-break promotion together with a group of local authorities, but later pulled out from the project (leaving the financial support behind) as it felt that this initiative was not one it wished to support.

Regional tourist boards have very wide and frequent contact with all sectors of the tourism industry within the region. This is achieved through several activities:

- publication of tourism strategies;
- distribution of newsletters;
- commercial members' meetings;
- tourism officers' meetings;
- running training courses;
- giving advice;
- supporting or instigating joint initiatives.

All tourist boards carry out a range of marketing activities, which include the following.

Publications

Most boards publish a range of items:

- main guide — a general promotional item in magazine format, usually for sale, often with an accommodation listing;
- accommodation guides — various;
- attractions guide — either a broadsheet or a 'card system';
- conference guide — listing conference venues and hotels;
- group organisers' manual — for tour operators and other group organisers;
- events leaflet;
- special interest leaflets — usually relatively simply produced, with information for hobbyists.

The above items are distributed in a variety of ways

by direct mail, through tourist information centres, newsagents, and at public and trade exhibitions.

Advertising

Adverts usually carry general messages about the region or one or more aspects of the region's products. Adverts are usually placed through advertising agencies, are targeted towards particular consumers and are often linked to a wider promotional campaign.

Public relations

All boards host journalist trips and send out press releases. Journalist visits are sometimes instigated by the national boards or overseas offices of the BTA, and at other times by the regional tourist boards or by journalists themselves. Releases are usually prepared and mailed in-house.

Exhibitions

All boards attend trade exhibitions and public exhibitions in the UK and overseas.

Joint promotions

All boards take part in these with each other, with other organisations and with the commercial sector.

Direct mail

All boards are involved in direct mail exercises. Names and addresses are often compiled from previous enquirers and visitors. Mailing lists are occasionally purchased.

Targeting

All boards target their marketing activities, and all target a range of market segments, with actual segments targeted being subject to the nature of the product, traditional holiday markets for the region and other factors.

The regional tourist boards target their marketing in the following ways.

- **By holiday type**
  - main holiday (four nights or more),
  - short holiday or short-break,
  - business tourism,
  - visits to friends and relatives.

- **By geography**
  - often to traditional markets,
  - often to residents of South East England,
  - other conurbations,
  - overseas short-haul,
  - overseas long-haul.

- **By socio-economic group or lifestyle, including**
  - over 40s with children left home,
  - under 35s with no children,
  - young families on a budget,
  - second and subsequent time overseas visitors.

Monitoring

All boards monitor their activities to some extent. This usually includes accurate monitoring of responses generated by advertising and direct mail exercises. However, boards are not in a position to allocate more of their scarce resources to this area.

The boards also operate press-cutting services to monitor the results of their own PR activity and to gain a general picture of messages relating to the region.

Summary

- **Regional tourist boards are responsible for the marketing of a whole region.**
- **They are well aware of the dual objectives of the national parks.**
- **They use the national parks as unique selling points in their marketing, universally including scenic photographs of the parks in their print items. The term 'national park' is seen as a way of 'endorsing' the quality of landscapes in the area.**
- **The nature and quantity of consultation between the regional tourist boards and the NPAs varies from park to park (see section 12). Inconsistent messages from different national parks and from different individuals within NPAs lead to confusion.**
- **Regional tourist boards carry out wide and frequent consultation with the commercial sector of the tourism industry.**
- **The boards have a sophisticated marketing function and undertake a range of targeted marketing activities.**
- **Regional tourist boards monitor the results of their activities, but in general feel that more resources are needed in this area.**

10. TOURISM BUSINESSES OPERATING AT A DISTANCE FROM THE NATIONAL PARKS

Completed questionnaires were received from 27 tour and transport operators located at a distance from the national parks. Of these, 44 per cent operated tours to one or more national park(s).

Awareness of dual objectives

Of this group, 92 per cent were aware of the dual objectives of the national parks. The remaining 8 per cent thought that national park designation existed to conserve beautiful landscapes only.

Sales value of the national parks

In place of the 'location' question, operators were asked if tours to national parks were easier or more difficult to sell than tours that did not include national parks:
- 57 per cent said there was no difference;
- 33 per cent said tours to national parks were easier to sell;
- 10 per cent said tours to national parks were harder to sell.

Consultation for promotional advice

A higher level of consultation was recorded compared with businesses located in or near the national parks:
- 36 per cent consulted a regional tourist board;
- 21 per cent consulted a district council tourism department;
- 28 per cent did not consult;
- 15 per cent consulted other organisations.

This high level of consultation is to be expected since regional tourist boards and district councils target tour operators, and because it is likely that the operator initially collected information on the destination(s) in question from a regional tourist board or district council, either direct, or at an exhibition.

Type of promotional activities undertaken

These are similar to tourism businesses in and near national parks, with most operators engaged in production and distribution of promotional print (58 per cent) and advertising (75 per cent). Displaying posters and signboards was more important to coach operators.

Target markets

Day trippers were the most commonly targeted group, but the result is biased by responses from transport and coach operators. The sample size is not large enough to draw conclusions about the activities of different types of operator.

Target market	(%)
Main holiday tourists	18
Short-break tourists	12
Overseas visitors	18
Visitors in park	5
Day trippers	41
Other or none	6

Monitoring of success

Tour and transport operators far from national parks carried out less monitoring than businesses in or near national parks. This figure is again distorted by the coach operator content of the sample. The majority (85 per cent) of tour and transport operators carry out no monitoring.

Promotional success

Despite the low level of monitoring, operators were not especially disappointed by the results of their promotion, with 89 per cent of the sample selecting either answer 2 or 3 on the scale (with 1 denoting most successful and 5 denoting least successful).

II. ORGANISATIONS OPERATING AT AN INTERNATIONAL AND NATIONAL LEVEL

This section consists of a summary of interviews with organisations operating at an international and national level.

The British Tourist Authority

At the international level, marketing of the national parks to overseas tourists falls under the activities of the British Tourist Authority (BTA). BTA's remit is to promote the whole of Britain to overseas visitors.

The BTA sees the national parks as 'a valuable tourist draw', and understands the need to 'balance' visitor numbers in the parks.

The BTA consults the Countryside Commission at a national level during all work that involves the English and Welsh countryside, although there appears to be no formal structure or consultation criteria by which overseas BTA officers consult the national parks themselves.

The BTA is aware that the British countryside is a major attraction for overseas visitors, and sees the national parks as one element of that 'product'. The British countryside as a whole has a much higher profile than the national parks among overseas visitors to Britain.

London is by far the most popular UK destination among first and second time visitors to Britain. The BTA tries to encourage second and subsequent time visitors to other destinations, including the countryside.

Promotional activities

The BTA's main promotional activity is print production and distribution. It produces over 50 publications, ranging from glossy brochures to simple information sheets. Publications tend to be 'global', with each overseas office selecting the publications most relevant to their territory.

The national parks feature in a number of publications, but there is no apparent pattern or policy direction to their mention or use.

Publications

The BTA's annual main promotional guide for Britain is produced in 14 language versions and 25 geographic editions, with a circulation of 1.8 million world-wide. Each version has its own particular emphasis; the national parks are referred to in various contexts.

For example, *Britain is great* is the German version, and mentions the parks under a number of sections, including 'activities' and 'regional breakdown'. The countryside in general has a higher profile in this tourist market and the publication reflects this. *Britain for all seasons* is the North American version, which concentrates more on the urban environment, with sections on 'London', 'great towns' and 'picturesque villages'. The national parks are referred to less often.

Another BTA publication is *Piece by piece*, which was initially designed to help overseas visitors organise their trips around Britain. References to the parks include a photograph, promotion of operators that feature park areas, and in-passing reference to the parks.

Two BTA publications, *Britain's Treasured Landscapes* and *Walking in Britain*, feature the national parks in particular.

Britain's Treasured Landscapes

BTA's contribution to *Britain's Treasured Landscapes* was 30 per cent of the funding (with the remainder provided by the Countryside Commission and British Petroleum). It was produced in response to increasing demand from potential overseas visitors for information on the British countryside. The BTA sees it as a useful and effective information tool, and feels that it has been well received by the overseas offices.

Walking in Britain

This publication features 59 walks in and around Britain. The national parks are referred to extensively, especially pictorially.

It is impossible to quantify exactly the extent to which these and the other BTA publications feature, mention or promote the national parks. Most of BTA's publications concentrate on a particular product, for example accommodation, or coach tours, many of which refer to one or more of the national parks.

Other activities

A number of activities are carried out in parallel with print production; the most relevant to national parks are described below.

Posters are produced for distribution through BTA's overseas offices, at exhibitions, promotions, etc. Some of these feature scenes of the British countryside.

BTA works closely with the media in overseas countries to encourage press coverage of British holidays. Visits are arranged for overseas travel and holiday journalists to Britain; these are normally unaccompanied — the journalists are simply supplied with a car and a proposed itinerary. Other visits are in small groups, usually planned with the help of a regional board.

The *Britain Calling* magazine is produced monthly and distributed from BTA's overseas offices. This contains occasional features on the countryside or the national parks.

The BTA monitors coverage of Britain in the overseas press; clipping is managed and used by the overseas offices.

English Tourist Board

The ETB's marketing and development departments are aware of problems of visitor pressure in national parks, and are also aware that these vary considerably from park to park. The ETB takes this situation into account during the planning and implementation of its marketing; it treats the national parks as a special case because of their sensitivity.

Promotion of the national parks by the ETB tends to occur 'coincidentally', as part of a wider destination- or product-based promotion, rather than in a specific way.

ETB produces a range of publications, some of which, like its main *England* brochure, are intended for a very general audience, while others, for example *Let's Go*, are more clearly targeted. There are four types of publications:

- campaign publications for general image building;
- joint publications produced jointly with the trade, for example *Caravan holidays*, and publications that are supported by trade contributions;
- product publications, for example *Activity holidays*;
- commercial publications, which include directories and guides, for example *Stay on a farm* and the *Where to stay* guides.

ETB carries out limited advertising and this is linked to campaigns. Public relations is given a higher priority and is closely linked to campaigns. Specific activities include publication of the *Grosvenor Clarion*, which is mailed monthly to travel journalists and editors.

ETB sets up and coordinates development initiatives known as Tourism Development Action Programmes (TDAPs). A number of these have run or are currently running. They are sub-regional *foci* for tourism development and marketing and are usually funded jointly by ETB, the relevant regional tourist board, the local authorities, other funding agencies and the commercial sector. Two of these relate specifically to national parks — Dartmoor and Exmoor (see section 12) — and others have occurred close to or in part overlapping national parks, for example the Kielder TDAP, Norwich TDAP and the Eden valley TDAP.

ETB plays a coordinating role for organisations lower down the tourism hierarchy and organises its own annual travel trade exhibition, 'Moot'.

ETB issues no specific marketing messages relating to the national parks in its publications, but at interview stated that it tries to demonstrate consideration and awareness of the national park situation, especially in the Lake District where visitor pressure problems are particularly severe.

There is no formal consultation mechanism on promotional activities between the marketing department of ETB and the national parks or the Countryside Commission, but the department would contact one or the other should it feel unsure about an issue or the implications of an initiative.

There are currently no clear specific policies or guide-lines for marketing the national parks that ETB's marketing department feels it can follow. The Joint Heads of Agreement and the *Principles for tourism in the national parks* provide a framework and a policy direction, but no specific guide-lines for promotion of the national parks.

Wales Tourist Board

The Wales Tourist Board (WTB) views the three Welsh national parks as important elements of the Welsh tourism product, going so far as to describe them as 'gems in our crown' and 'vitally important in the Board's marketing plans'. The WTB is aware of the need for sensitivity in promotion of the national parks and is aware of national park objectives; WTB does not feel that these cause problems for marketing. WTB is aware of potential conflict over specific tourism developments, is a contributing member of the Heads of Agreement on national parks and has agreed to the *Principles for tourism in the national parks*.

Marketing by WTB is broken down into a number of products (for example activity holidays and short breaks) and some of these are further broken down by region. Regions do not relate to national park boundaries. Photography of national park landscapes is frequently used in promotional print, and the term 'national park' is used to infer 'quality' and 'importance' of landscapes.

WTB's advertising concentrates on the branding of Wales as a destination. Products are sometimes featured, but generally not sub-national destinations.

Individual and group journalist visits are often taken into national parks; WTB advises them of the sensitivity of national parks.

WTB prints a series of 12 posters, three of which show scenes in national parks. The Pembrokeshire National Park Authority objected to one, showing a beach on the Pembrokeshire coast, but WTB went ahead with production and distribution as the Board felt that it would not have a detrimental effect.

WTB has only 'rare' contact with national park authorities, and feels that consultation on marketing issues should be more frequent. The Board feels that the national park authorities are unwilling to engage in such consultation. An example quoted by WTB of this was the initial consultation during the National Parks Awareness Campaign, concerning WTB's willingness to part-fund and produce a print item about the three national parks. Lack of response from the national park authorities resulted in the failure of the project.

The Countryside Commission

The Countryside Commission, which has as one of its objectives to 'promote public enjoyment of the countryside' has, as a result of this objective, a marketing remit — although for the countryside in general and not just for the national parks.

Marketing as a management technique has in the past been given a relatively low priority by the Commission. The Commission now feels that it needs to embrace the technique more fully, and has recently taken a secondee from Shell to advise on marketing and to develop marketing strategies for a number of its activities. Marketing is a function of the activities of a number of departments and individuals; 'Communications Branch' and 'Recreation and Access Branch' seem to be the most active in the field of marketing.

Most of the literature produced and distributed by the Commission to date has concentrated on:
- promoting policies for the countryside;
- providing information about the countryside.

The majority of Commission publications are targeted towards the organisations with which the Commission is working, or hoping to work, in its enabling and advisory roles, such as land owners, government organisations, farmers, and local authorities.

The Commission's message regarding the national parks is that 'they are some of our finest landscapes, they are fragile and they need to be cared for'.

Publications relating to visitors and national parks include the following.
- A series of national park guide books which provide factual information on geology, natural history, landscape, history. These explain some of the pressures on the national parks and list places of interest, useful addresses, etc. Each carries a message regarding the importance of, and reasons for, national parks in the form of a letter from the Chairman of the Commission.
- A series of guides to the national trails are produced in cooperation with the Ordnance Survey and Aurum Press. Some of the trails pass through national parks.
- A series of posters is published, one poster for each national park. These carry a photograph of a landscape characteristic of the national park and the name of the park followed by the tag 'a national park'. The posters are on sale from the Commission by mail order and from a limited number of outlets in national parks. These were first published as part of the awareness campaign, but have been retained as they are commercially successful.
- The Commission recently jointly published *Britain's Treasured Landscapes*. This A5, full-colour booklet is available in five languages including English. It briefly describes each national park, along with scenic areas in Scotland. It shows sources of further information and travelling times to the national parks by rail from London and 'gateway' railway stations. It also describes the YHA, the National Trust, BTCV holidays and rail-rover tickets available overseas and in Britain. It carries the country code and a message from the Chairman of the Commission that invites the reader to visit the 'treasured landscapes of Britain' and advises that they need to be respected and carefully treated. Distribution of the booklet is mainly by BTA through its overseas offices and at overseas exhibitions and trade fairs.

The Commission consults the national park authorities on all activities it carries out that relate to the parks.

Summary

- **The British Tourist Authority, the English and Wales Tourist Boards and the Countryside Commission are the organisations concerned with marketing at the international and national level.**
- **The national tourist boards market Britain, England and Wales as whole products. They use the national parks as unique selling points.**
- **These are sophisticated marketing organisations that carry out a number of activities, some of which relate to national parks.**
- **The national tourist boards are aware of the sensitivity of tourism in national parks and consult with the Countryside Commission or individual NPAs on initiatives in national parks.**
- ***Britain's Treasured Landscapes* is the first print item dedicated to the promotion of all of the national parks. It is used mainly for overseas promotion.**

A number of formal consultation groups or fora exist in or near to national park areas. These have been formed for a variety of reasons, but all have been formed in response to the uncoordinated nature of tourism marketing and the lack of communication between organisations in specific national park areas. Three brief examples are described below.

Dartmoor TDAP

The Tourism Development Action Programme (TDAP) started following pressure from the local tourism association, which felt that marketing of the area was being duplicated by several local authorities and other organisations. At the same time, the NPA and the three main district councils felt that tourism could make a greater contribution both to visitor enjoyment and to the local economy if marketing efforts were coordinated more effectively.

The TDAP was set up in April 1986 with specific objectives to:
- protect and enhance the basic resources upon which the tourist industry is based;
- identify and develop opportunities for maintaining and increasing the contribution that tourism makes to the local economy;
- minimise any potential adverse effects of tourism upon local communities.

A full-time officer was appointed and was made responsible for leading and coordinating action.

Funding for the TDAP was generated from the Dartmoor National Park, three district councils, Devon County Council, West Country Tourist Board and the Dartmoor Tourist Association.

Marketing activities undertaken include:
- production of an accommodation guide and bed booking service;
- production of an information/advice leaflet for local tourism businesses;
- production of a leaflet entitled *The secret villages of the Dartmoor area*, which encourages visitors to visit villages on the edge of the national park area.

A number of committees have been set up to direct the TDAP; the NPA chairs the officers' working party, which submits reports to the TDAP steering group.

Success

The NPA feels that the TDAP acts as the main consultation medium for the Dartmoor area and has started to bring the marketing activities of various organisations together. The NPA has an influential role in the decision making process of the programme group, and feels that the group's activities have been consistent with the aims of the park. In the four years of its operation, the TDAP has not lost any of its funding partners, which implies a successful operation. However, as with all fora, there are inherent tensions between the partners.

Peak District Forum

Centred on the Peak District National Park, the forum was a response to the duplication of tourism marketing in and around the park; this was especially noticeable in the Peak District, where 12 local authorities, four tourist boards and a number of other organisations are involved in tourism marketing.

The Peak District Forum was set up in 1987. It essentially operates as a working party and a consultation forum for public sector organisations. Its major promotional activity is the annual production of the *Peak District Holidays* brochure, which carries advertising from tourism organisations and businesses in the area, and is distributed nationally. The East Midlands Tourist Board coordinates production and distribution.

Success

The forum has brought together all public sector organisations in the area and has provided a consultation platform. The brochure is felt to be successful, but the forum has yet to meet its objectives of coordinating tourism promotional activities fully. A number of authorities continue to promote their own particular part of the area, which divides the park in terms of tourism promotion.

Members interviewed for this study suggested that the forum was unstable and the threat of collapse constant because of the large number of authorities and their often conflicting objectives. The forum is attempting to involve the private sector in its organisation, and the appointment of an officer to coordinate future activities has been suggested.

The Peak District Forum is an attempt to deal with a difficult and unique tourism marketing situation.

Exmoor Tourism Advisory Group

This forum was set up after the completion of the Exmoor TDAP in order to maintain the interest of, and cooperation between, the TDAP partners. According to members interviewed for the study, the TDAP was an effective consultation forum that encouraged dialogue between all of the organisations promoting the Exmoor area. The Advisory Group continues this consultation process.

The local tourism association plays an important role in the consultaton process and leads many of the joint activities that promote the area; the *Exmoor for enchanting holidays* brochure, for example, has attempted to bring a number of organisations together in order to unify promotion.

All organisations interviewed felt that the Group served an important role as a consultation platform.

Summary

- Consultation fora exist in Dartmoor, Exmoor and the Peak District. These have tourism marketing objectives.
- These consultation fora are slightly different in nature, in order to take account of local conditions.
- The Dartmoor TDAP was set up most recently. This initiative has an area of interest that is wider than the national park boundary. Its objectives are consistent with national park aims.
- All three suffer from tensions that are the result of differences in the partners' objectives. This fact is detrimental to the objective of the fora to coordinate the marketing of the national park area.
- The Peak District Forum, which has the highest number of members, is the least stable and the least effective.

In order to evaluate the messages relating to national parks that are communicated by businesses and organisations, respondents were asked to return a copy of their promotional literature with their completed questionnaire. More than half (55 per cent) returned promotional literature with their questionnaire.

The literature was read and the messages contained were judged against a check-list, as follows.

Level one

Mention of the national park. *Informal mention* — ie, mention of the geographical area, for example, 'The Lakes' or 'Lakeland'. *Formal mention* — ie, 'The Lake District National Park'.

Level two

Mention of the special character of the area.

Level three

Mention of four 'deeper' messages:
- enjoyment of the area/national park;
- appreciation of the area/national park;
- understanding of the area/national park;
- concern for the area/national park.

The results are summarised in Table 8.

Just under half of those returning literature mentioned a national park in a way that was measurable on the scale.

The simpler messages of level one were mentioned most frequently; frequency of mention decreased with increasing complexity of the message to a point where less than 1 per cent mentioned concern for a national park.

Generally, messages relating to national parks are given low priority in promotional literature, being clearly secondary to messages relating to the specific product or service that the print item is promoting. For example, most hotel brochures concentrate on the facilities available, the decor and the cooking, followed by those describing location, views, etc, the national park sometimes featuring formally or informally at this point.

Formal national park mentions were frequently made in order to suggest that a high scenic quality exists at a destination, in particular those mentions that appeared in local authority or tourist board literature.

Messages that referred to a unique selling point (such as Hadrian's Wall in Northumberland, or Lorna Doone in Exmoor) were more frequent than messages referring to the national park.

No messages contrary to national park objectives were monitored. Few of the messages monitored could be said to be in accordance with national park objectives; most did not take these into account.

Table 8. *Nature of treatment of the national parks in promotional literature by organisations and businesses.*

Message	All organisations and businesses in and near to the national parks	Organisations and businesses in the national parks	Organisations and businesses near to the national parks
Make no mention at all	29	24	44
Mention the park by name	17	20	13
Mention the name of the geographical area	19	19	18
Mention the special character of the area	6	6	1
Mention enjoyment of the national park	21	23	16
Mention appreciation of the national park	5	6	5
Mention understanding of the national park	2	1	2
Mention concern for the national park	1	1	1

Summary

- **Messages relating to the national parks are given a low priority in promotional print by both businesses and organisations — less than half of those surveyed mentioned them in any way.**

- **Mention of more complex messages relating to 'understanding of' or 'concern for' the national parks is rare.**
- **The national parks are often used in promotional literature to infer a high quality of scenic beauty.**

14. FINANCE

The following is the total of promotional spending by businesses and organisations monitored by the consultants.

Table 9. Total promotional spending by businesses and other organisations.

	Businesses* (£)	Local authorities and regional tourist boards** (£)	National park authorities (£)
The Broads	891,700	102,000	not available
The Brecon Beacons	1,600,200	52,000	16,000
Dartmoor	1,119,450	150,000	21,000
The Yorkshire Dales	731,000	94,000	not available
Exmoor	1,029,300	115,000	not available
The Lake District	3,720,300	553,000	36,000
Northumberland	1,460,500	65,000	37,000
The North York Moors	2,091,000	105,000	not available
The Peak District	1,623,400	240,000	8,000
Pembrokeshire Coast	1,338,500	99,000	not available
Snowdonia	2,388,200	347,000	50,000
TOTAL	**17,993,550**	**1,922,000**	**168,000**

* Total promotional spend monitored by businesses located in and near to the national parks during the study.

** Actual promotional spend by local authorities monitored, plus a percentage proportion of regional tourist board spend based on a percentage of area covered by the national park.

Promotional spending by national park authorities proved to be very difficult to identify because national parks do not have 'marketing' or 'promotion' budgets and marketing activities are often allocated to a number of budget heads. Figures that the consultants were able to identify are shown above. The following notes should be applied to the above total figure.

The database represents between approximately 50 and 70 per cent of the total number of businesses operating in and near the national parks, marketing by which will result in visits to the national parks. The figure for spend by businesses shown above, then, should be subject to this factor:

$$£17,993,550 \times \frac{100}{70} = £25,705,071$$

A proportion of spending by the BTA, ETB and WTB will result in visits to the parks, but this is further removed and even more difficult to calculate. The following is considered to be a 'reasonable estimate' by the consultants.

	Marketing budget (£)		(%)		(£)
British Tourist Authority	25.5 m*	×	1	=	255,000
English Tourist Board	3.7 m**	×	2	=	74,000
Wales Tourist Board	2.5 m	×	5	=	125,000
					454,000

* This is BTA's total budget, excluding contributions to print and projects by other organisations.

** This is ETB's marketing budget, which is expenditure plus salaries minus income.

The extrapolated figure for promotional spending by businesses and organisations that results in visits to national parks is approximately as follows.

Businesses	£25,705,071
Local authorities and proportion of regional tourist board spend	£1,922,000
Proportion of national tourist board spend	£454,000
Approximate national park authority spend	£168,000
	£28,249,071

The consultants estimate that total promotional spend by the tourism industry in England and Wales is approximately £300,000,000, so the spending identifed in national parks represents about eight per cent.

Data collected from organisations contained some inconsistencies; in particular, some local authorities included the cost of operating tourist information centres in marketing budgets (as this was seen as a promotional activity) while others did not.

Staff and support costs are omitted from the local authority and regional tourist boards promotional budgets. If these were included, the figure of £1,922,000 could be doubled.

The figure above does not include the value of editorial exposure achieved by tourism organisations and businesses. The consultants estimate that this figure could be in the region of £30,000,000.

The Northumbria Tourist Board, one of the smaller boards, monitored £930,000 of coverage for the region during 1989. With a total of nine regional tourist boards, two national boards, the British Tourist Authority and 50 local authorities engaged in this activity, this figure of £30 million could be conservative.

Summary

- Total promotional spend by business and organisations is approximately as follows:
  — £25,705,071 by businesses;
  — £1,922,000 by local authorities and regional tourist boards;
  — £454,000 by national bodies;
  — £168,000 by national park authorities.

Promotional spending on national parks is approximately 8 per cent of total tourism promotional spend in England and Wales.

15. RECOMMENDATIONS: MARKETING

All national parks should appoint a tourism officer.

- Businesses, local authorities and tourist boards will continue to market tourism to the national parks; most national park authorities have little or no influence on this activity. A national park tourism officer would work with these organisations to encourage them to carry out marketing that is consistent with national park aims.

- A tourism officer would be a focus for all tourism-related communication and would help to overcome the current situation in which different individual national park staff communicate conflicting messages to the same outside organisations.

- A tourism officer would be able to encourage more joint marketing activities, which would give an opportunity to introduce more national park messages into tourism promotion.

National parks should encourage the setting up of partnerships with regional tourist boards and local tourism businesses.

- This would enable the national parks to extend their sphere of activity and influence beyond their boundaries, leading to more effective visitor management and a tourism industry that is more aware of, and consistent with, national park aims.

National park staff should be given marketing training.

- This will enable national park staff to better understand and make use of marketing as a management technique.

- The training should concentrate on the marketing of tourism businesses and organisations, their special requirements and the nature of the tourism industry.

The national parks should be promoted in a corporate way.

- All parks are individually communicating the message that each is special, fragile and needs special protection. Considerable benefits (increased penetration, enhanced value, economies of scale, etc) could be gained from a 'corporate' communications exercise.

- Elements of this exercise might be:
  — a consistent graphic framework for all national park print;
  — a message on all national park print linking each to a family — 'one of the eleven national parks of England & Wales';
  — a pro-active public relations campaign to communicate the corporate message.

The national parks should have a consistent policy on, and consistent objectives for, merchandising.

- All of the national parks are engaged in merchandising, although level of activity, level of expertise and objectives vary.

- The national parks would benefit considerably (as did the Forestry Commission recently) if:
  — merchandising were given clear objectives;
  — a central buying facility were to be introduced;
  — clear stocking, margin and buying policies were introduced.

The national parks should make better use of public relations.

- With their relatively low marketing budgets, the national parks would be well advised to put more professionalism and resources into their public relations effort.

- The national parks should communicate pro-actively (rather than the predominantly re-active situation that currently applies) by building relationships with journalists, regularly sending press releases in a planned way, and hosting journalists in a planned way.

- Press clipping procedures should be made more effective and should be used to monitor media messages.

The effectiveness and role of national park newspapers should be reviewed.

- Although all of the national parks claim to produce only 'quality' publications, all but three produce a newspaper, which cannot be considered to be a quality print item.

- The newspapers are expected to perform a multi-purpose function:
  — providing information on what to do (for visitors who are already in or close to a park);
  — acting as an accommodation guide;
  — carrying national park messages.

- National park authorities do not know if these functions are being effectively achieved through the newspaper medium.

- The newspapers may be trying to perform too many roles, and have been adopted by national parks as a communications medium because they are cheap to produce.

- A study of users of the newspapers should be carried out to evaluate this medium against its objectives, to establish the newspapers' effectiveness and the images of national parks that are communicated to visitors through them.

Resources available to the national park authorities for marketing should be reviewed in the light of these recommendations.

16. CONSERVATION SUPPORT SURVEY

Four questions were added to the marketing questionnaire in order to collect information on:

- how many organisations give support to conservation projects in the national park;
- what form that support takes;
- which types of conservation benefit;
- which conservation organisations benefit;
- whether existing levels of support were likely to fall, stay the same or increase.

From the responses received, it appeared that 25 per cent of businesses gave some kind of support to conservation projects and 75 per cent gave no support.

There was little variation in the level of support by location and by business type, although businesses located in national parks recorded a slightly higher level of support than those located near to national parks, and a higher proportion of activity centres gave support than attraction or accommodation operators.

The proportion of businesses giving support varied considerably from park to park (from 16 per cent in Dartmoor to 39 per cent in the Brecon Beacons).

What did they give?

Figure 8. Percentage of businesses giving different kinds of support for conservation.

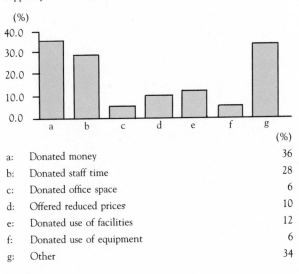

		(%)
a:	Donated money	36
b:	Donated staff time	28
c:	Donated office space	6
d:	Offered reduced prices	10
e:	Donated use of facilities	12
f:	Donated use of equipment	6
g:	Other	34

Which organisations benefited?

Most businesses that gave support to conservation projects said that they carried out the conservation project themselves.

Analysis of the comments made by respondents in this group revealed three general segments within the group.

- Those who feel that the operation of their business is an act of conservation in itself (by supporting the community, by keeping a location tidy, or in one case 'by adding hanging baskets'!).

Figure 9. Which organisations benefited from the donations?

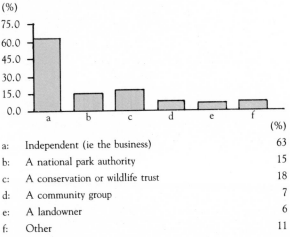

		(%)
a:	Independent (ie the business)	63
b:	A national park authority	15
c:	A conservation or wildlife trust	18
d:	A community group	7
e:	A landowner	6
f:	Other	11

- Those who supply national park information leaflets to their guests, or verbally explain the sensitivity and special nature of the park to guests (mainly activity centres and accommodation providers).
- Those (a tiny minority) who carry out major projects on their land (for example 'buying four acres of land and creating a wetland' and 'having power lines laid underground across the property at a cost of £10,000').

After businesses themselves, conservation trusts and then national park authorities were the most common recipients of support. The actual proportions varied considerably from park to park, and were very much dependent on local conditions and the level of activity by different groups (see appendix 4).

What type of project was supported?

Projects relating to trees received the highest support, followed by projects involving footpaths. There was much variation from park to park (see appendix 4); for example, footpath projects were supported more by businesses in the Peak District and the Lake District (50 per cent and 41 per cent respectively) where footpath erosion has a high profile. Footpath projects, however, received surprisingly little support in the Yorkshire Dales (22 per cent), despite the high profile of the Three Peaks and Pennine Way footpath erosion problems.

Will the level of support change?

Very few of the businesses that already gave support expected their support to reduce, and over a third of businesses expected their level of support to increase

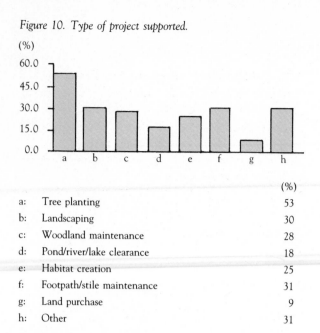

Figure 10. Type of project supported.

		(%)
a:	Tree planting	53
b:	Landscaping	30
c:	Woodland maintenance	28
d:	Pond/river/lake clearance	18
e:	Habitat creation	25
f:	Footpath/stile maintenance	31
g:	Land purchase	9
h:	Other	31

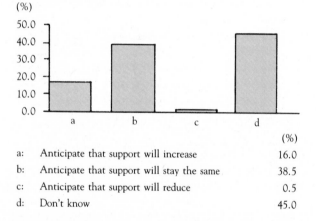

Figure 11. Businesses' anticipated level of change for conservation support.

		(%)
a:	Anticipate that support will increase	16.0
b:	Anticipate that support will stay the same	38.5
c:	Anticipate that support will reduce	0.5
d:	Don't know	45.0

(those already giving and new givers). However, the most interesting statistic is the 45 per cent who did not know whether their level of support would change.

Analysis of the comments received reveal a very high incidence of unprompted requests from businesses for more information on how to support conservation in national parks. Typical comments were:

- 'Would be willing to help if asked';
- 'Would like to know how to help';
- 'Would like to contribute to the national park but don't have any information on how to do so';
- 'Have never been approached for help'.

Few pro-active fundraising projects specific to national parks were found during this survey. However, the following two examples are worthy of note.

- The Exmoor hotelier who imposes a 25 pence per person per night levy on all bills, the funds collected being donated to the county conservation trust.
- 'The farmland trees project' introduced by Ryedale District Council, under which residents and tourists are invited to 'buy' a tree that will be planted by the side of one of a number of designated 'green roads' in the district.

Tourist boards gave little or no support to conservation projects in national parks. Local authorities gave support in some cases, but this was not channelled through tourism departments or officers, and so was not monitored.

Summary

- **Three-quarters (75 per cent) of businesses give no support whatsoever to conservation projects.**
- **Only 2 per cent of businesses give financial support.**
- **About two-thirds (63 per cent) of the businesses that give manage their own projects.**
- **Many businesses feel that they are supporting conservation in a national park simply by operating their business.**
- **Woodland and footpath projects are the most commonly supported types of conservation project.**
- **Many businesses would support conservation projects, but do not know how to, or have not been asked to do so.**

17. RECOMMENDATIONS: CONSERVATION

The conservation support survey shows that the level of support for conservation from tourism businesses is very low. It also shows that a proportion of businesses (unknown, but possibly substantial) would be prepared to support conservation projects if they were given information on how to do so. The following recommendations are made in order to take advantage of this situation.

The national parks should initiate schemes to attract tourism resources into conservation work.

- National park authorities should take the lead in bringing together all conservation organisations working in the national parks, on a park by park basis, into national park conservation panels.
- The panels should draw up lists of projects in need of funding.
- The panels should then promote funding opportunities to businesses located in and near to the national parks by means of the production and distribution of a leaflet and, if resources and expertise are available, through a park-wide promotional campaign of press releases and possibly events.

- To give businesses more encouragement to give support, a logo and slogan should be developed. The right to display this on literature, doorways, advertising, etc, would then be given only to businesses that support the scheme.

The national parks should initiate public conservation support schemes.

- After a network of participating businesses is established, it would be possible to build on this by involving these businesses and other outlets (such as tourist information centres) in raising resources for conservation projects from visitors to the national parks.
- This would involve the development of schemes under which interested visitors could make donations to conservation (the farmland trees project is an example and could be a useful model).
- It would be made more effective by collecting the names and addresses of contributors on a database that would allow direct mail fund-raising appeals in subsequent years.
- From this, a national database of visitors to national parks who are committed to supporting national parks could be developed and may prove to be a useful marketing tool, not only for conservation support.

Introduction

The most beautiful and unspoilt expanses of countryside in England and Wales have been designated national parks. The dual purposes of national park status are to preserve and enhance natural beauty and to provide for public enjoyment.

Tourism is an important part of the life of national parks. It brings a sense of refreshment and well-being to visitors; it helps the rural economy through support for income and jobs and it also maintains services in many national park communities. Yet tourism can bring with it damage to the fabric and wildlife of the countryside.

The future of tourism in national parks is ultimately dependent on their high quality natural environments. Where the natural beauty of the national parks and tourism is in irreconcilable conflict, then the former must prevail. The tourism industry's own actions need to support the protection of national parks and help sustain their environmental qualities. The natural beauty of the national parks must be unimpaired for the enjoyment of this and future generations.

Principles for tourism in national parks

The Countryside Commission and the English Tourist Board believe that tourism in national parks needs to be guided and judged by *all* of these principles, if it is to meet tourists' needs and protect national parks both now and in the future.

1. Conservation

The tourism industry can help to protect the distinctive landscapes and wildlife of national parks by supporting practical conservation measures. This can be achieved, for example, through joint initiatives involving the public, private and voluntary sectors.

2. Enjoyment

The activities and interests promoted by tourism should draw on the special character of the national parks, with their many opportunities for quiet open air recreation and their distinctive beauty, culture, history and wildlife. Improved access for visitors should be sought where this is compatible with conservation requirements.

3. Rural economy

The social and economic well-being of the residents of the national parks is an essential consideration in achieving the statutory objectives of national parks, and employment in the tourist and related service industries is an important part of the economy of the national parks. The tourism industry should support the economy of local communities through, for example, using employees, products and services from the locality and by supporting the skills and economic activities that are traditional to national parks.

4. Development

Appropriate facilities are needed to enable tourists to enjoy the national parks. All tourism development must respect the quality of the landscape and environment in national parks. Its scale, in particular, must always be appropriate to the setting. It should also recognise that some areas of national parks are valued for being wild and remote. Proposals for development should always be tempered by the capacity of the immediate site and surrounding landscape to absorb visitors. Development can assist the purposes of conservation and recreation by, for example, bringing sympathetic new uses to historic buildings and derelict sites and opening up new opportunities for quiet open-air recreation.

5. Design

The scale, siting, planning, design and management of new tourism developments should be in keeping with the landscape, and should seek to enhance it. The distinctive and highly valued character and landscapes of national parks will continue to evolve through small-scale changes. Major alterations to the landscape are unacceptable.

6. Marketing

The tourism industry should use the publicity, information and marketing opportunities to deepen people's enjoyment, appreciation, understanding and concern for national parks.

Principles for tourism in the national parks, 1989, published by the Countryside Commission and English Tourist Board.

Objectives of joint action

The Countryside Commission and the English Tourist Board will collaborate to implement a range of initiatives relating to tourism in national parks. This work will be guided by the following objectives:

1. To promote the adoption by others of the *Principles for tourism in national parks*.
2. To encourage good practice in the tourist industry in national parks that embraces these principles.
3. To gain a better understanding of the nature and trends of tourism in the national parks and the views and aspirations of visitors.
4. To enhance people's awareness of the distinctive experience offered by a visit to a national park and the need for activities to be compatible with its conservation.
5. To encourage closer cooperation between those involved in tourism and the national park authorities.

APPENDIX 2. RESPONSE RATES TO THE QUESTIONNAIRE

Size of database and response rate by national park

National park	Total	Returned	Return rate (%)
All	5,884	1,446	25
Brecon Beacons	242	46	19
The Broads	348	118	34
Dartmoor	453	123	27
Exmoor	346	98	28
Lake District	1,119	285	25
Northumberland	432	96	22
North York Moors	885	207	23
Peak District	348	98	28
Pembrokeshire Coast	643	154	24
Snowdonia	636	98	15
Yorkshire Dales	432	123	28

Response numbers by location and by organisation type

	A	B	C	D	E	F	G	H	Other	Total by location
In a national park	680	40	143	0	16	8	15	12		914
Near a national park	306	19	47	0	14	22	5	13		426
Total by organisation type	986	59	190	0	30	30	20	25	106	1,446

A : Accommodation
B : Activity managers
C : Attractions
D : Land owners
E : Tour operators
F : Transport operators
G : Services
H : Voluntary countryside organisations

National organisations

Countryside Commission
Contact: Calvin Pugsley, Head of Communications

Wales Tourist Board
Contact: Wyn Mears, UK Marketing Director

English Tourist Board
Contact: David Phillips, Marketing (Product)

British Tourist Authority
Contact: Jane Michael, Marketing (Product) Executive

Brecon Beacons

Brecknock Borough Council
Contact: Sally Wookey, Tourism Officer

South Wales Tourism Council
Contact: Elen Pierce

National Park Office
Contact: Roger Stevens

Dartmoor

Devon County Council
Contact: Alan Clarke, Tourism Officer

West Country Tourist Board
Contact: Nigel Buckler

National Park Office
Contact: Dr Nick Atkinson

Dartmoor TDAP
Contact: Karen Lloyd

Exmoor

Somerset County Council
Contact: Roger Gouldsworthy

West Somerset District Council
Contact: Tim King

West Country Tourist Board
Contact: Nigel Buckler

National Park Office
Contact: Gerry Belton

Exmoor Tourism Association
Contact: Donald Wade

Lake District

South Lakeland District Council
Contact: Jim Walker, Tourism Officer

Cumbria Tourist Board
Contact: Andrew Maxted

Eden District Council
Contact: Mr Morgan, Tourism Officer

National Park Office
Contact: Peter Freeman

North York Moors

Ryedale District Council
Contact: Ginny Wick

Yorkshire and Humberside Tourist Board
Contact: Bob Collier

Richmondshire District Council
Contact: Mrs J R Lincoln-Taylor

National Park Office
Contact: Bill Breakell

Northumberland

Tynedale District Council
Contact: Lynn Turner

Northumbria Tourist Board
Contact: John Owen

National Park Office
Contact: Tony Hopkins/Mr A A Macdonald

Peak District

High Peak Borough Council
Contact: Linda Moon

East Midlands Tourist Board
Contact: Peter Allen

Yorkshire and Humberside Tourist Board
Contact: Bob Collier

North West Tourist Board
Contact: Frances Warrington

National Park Office
Contact: Roland Smith

Pembrokeshire Coast

Preseli Pembs. District Council
Contact: Richard Howells

South Wales Tourism Council
Contact: Elen Pierce

National Park Office
Contact: Peter Hordley

Snowdonia

Gwynedd County Council
Contact: Dr E Lloyd-Evans

North Wales Tourism Council
Contact: Ester Roberts

National Park Office
Contact: Marian Rees/Alan Jones

The Broads

East Anglia Tourist Board
Contact: Trevor Hayward

Norwich Area Tourism Agency
Contact: Paul Simons, Chief Executive

The Broads Authority
Contact: Jess Tunstall

Yorkshire Dales

Craven District Council
Contact: Peter Colley

Richmondshire District Council
Contact: Mrs J R Lincoln-Taylor

Cumbria Tourist Board
Contact: Andrew Maxted

South Lakeland District Council
Contact: Jim Walker

National Park Office
Contact: Philip Brown

APPENDIX 4. RESULTS OF THE CONSERVATION SUPPORT SURVEY

Breakdown by national park	Brecon Beacons (%)	Broads (%)	Dartmoor (%)	Exmoor (%)	Lake District (%)	Peak District (%)	Pembrokeshire (%)	Northumberland (%)	North York Moors (%)	Snowdonia (%)	Yorkshire Dales (%)
Percentage of businesses giving different kinds of support for conservation											
Donated money	7	8	6	7	19	6	6	9	5	11	4
Donated staff time	12	7	2	7	5	9	10	5	10	8	4
Donated office space	3	0	1	1	1	3	2	4	2	1	—
Offered reduced prices	3	0	1	—	3	1	5	4	2	7	2
Donated use of facilities	12	2	2	1	2	8	5	3	3	5	—
Equipment	3	1	0	0	1	4	4	1	3	0	—
None	61	81	84	77	68	79	71	81	80	66	79
Other	12	6	8	13	8	4	13	3	8	8	10
Percentage of businesses giving to projects managed by different organisations											
Independent	67	59	64	31	67	64	72	42	71	68	53
National park authority	11	6	7	15	16	36	9	0	21	16	21
Conservation or wildlife trust	11	18	7	8	18	27	31	33	18	11	5
Community group	0	12	14	23	9	9	3	0	3	11	5
Land owner	0	6	7	15	5	9	3	8	6	5	5
Other	22	18	21	23	11	9	3	17	3	11	16
Percentage of businesses supporting different kinds of conservation projects											
Tree planting	22	53	67	41	53	67	43	33	70	57	47
Landscaping	11	24	28	24	31	33	33	40	35	21	30
Woodland maintenance	11	30	14	29	24	25	16	27	51	36	30
Pond clearance	33	12	14	35	12	17	13	20	35	7	6
Habitat creation	11	18	19	24	26	33	17	33	43	7	26
Footpath work	11	24	29	35	41	50	23	27	27	36	22
Land purchase	11	0	10	18	2	33	7	6	16	7	9
Other	33	23	29	24	28	42	43	40	22	36	35
Anticipated level of change for conservation support											
Increase	21	17	12	15	13	12	19	22	17	23	15
No change	39	43	37	47	41	32	35	35	40	36	34
Reduce	0	7	0	0	0	0	0	0	1	0	1
Don't know	39	38	51	39	45	55	46	43	44	40	50

Printed by The Lavenham Press Limited, Lavenham, Suffolk, England.